# PRESIDENTS
## *of the* UNITED STATES

LEVEL **3** READER

GRADES 2 TO 4 · READING LEVEL

Written by Kathryn Knight
Features official White House portraits

bend⊕n®

## George Washington
## 1789–1797

**Vice President:** John Adams
**Political Party:** None
**State Represented:** Virginia
**Married:** Martha Custis
**Lived:** 1732–1799

General George Washington is called "The Father of His Country." As a general, he helped win the Revolutionary War. His face is on the one-dollar bill. Our Capital city is named after him.

## John Adams
## 1797–1801

**VP:** Thomas Jefferson
**Party:** Federalist
**State:** Massachusetts
**Married:** Abigail Smith
**Lived:** 1735–1826

John Adams is called "The Father of the Navy." He was the father of the 6th President. He was the first President to live in the White House. He died on July 4th—Independence Day!

### 3

## Thomas Jefferson
## 1801–1809

**VP:** Aaron Burr; George Clinton
**Party:** Democratic-Republican
**State:** Virginia
**Married:** Martha Skelton
**Lived:** 1743–1826

Thomas Jefferson was an excellent writer and thinker.
He wrote most of the Declaration of Independence.
He was a governor of Virginia. His face is on the nickel.
He died on July 4th, the same day as John Adams.

### 4

## James Madison
## 1809–1817

**VP:** George Clinton; Elbridge Gerry
**Party:** Democratic-Republican
**State:** Virginia
**Married:** Dolley Todd
**Lived:** 1751–1836

James Madison is called "The Father of the Bill of
Rights." He was the shortest President, at 5 feet 6 inches
tall.* He was a representative from Virginia. His face
is on the $5,000 bill—which is no longer used.

* According to historical records

### James Monroe
### 1817–1825
**VP:** Daniel D. Tompkins
**Party:** Democratic-Republican
**State:** Virginia
**Married:** Elizabeth Kortright
**Lived:** 1758 – 1831

James Monroe was a governor of Virginia. He implemented the Monroe Doctrine, which said that no European countries could try to colonize land in the Americas. He died on July 4th.

### John Quincy Adams
### 1825–1829
**VP:** John C. Calhoun
**Party:** Democratic-Republican
**State:** Massachusetts
**Married:** Louisa Johnson
**Lived:** 1767 – 1848

John Quincy Adams was the son of the 2nd President. He was the first former President to be photographed, in 1848. After his term, he served in Congress for 18 years.

## Andrew Jackson
## 1829–1837

**VP:** John C. Calhoun;
Martin Van Buren
**Party:** Democratic
**State:** Tennessee
**Married:** Rachel Donelson
**Lived:** 1767–1845

General Andrew Jackson was called "Old Hickory."
He was the very first representative from the state
of Tennessee. His face is on the 20-dollar bill.

## Martin Van Buren
## 1837–1841

**VP:** Richard M. Johnson
**Party:** Democratic
**State:** New York
**Married:** Hannah Hoes
**Lived:** 1782–1862

Martin Van Buren was a senator and governor from
New York. He was the only President who had to learn
English later in life. He grew up speaking Dutch.

### William Henry Harrison
**1841** (March 4–April 4)
**VP:** John Tyler
**Party:** Whig
**State:** Ohio
**Married:** Anna Symmes
**Lived:** 1773–1841

General William Harrison was the grandfather of the 23rd President. He was a senator from Ohio. He died in office of pneumonia, and served the shortest time of any President—only one month.

### John Tyler
**1841–1845**
**VP:** None
**Party:** Whig
**State:** Virginia
**Married:** Letitia Christian (d. 1842);
Julia Gardiner
**Lived:** 1790–1862

John Tyler was a governor and senator from Virginia. He became President after Harrison died. He was the first President to get married in office, and he was the father of 15 children!

### James Knox Polk
### 1845–1849

**VP:** George M. Dallas
**Party:** Democratic
**State:** Tennessee
**Married:** Sarah Childress
**Lived:** 1795–1849

James Polk was a governor and representative from Tennessee. While he was President, the boundaries of the territories of the United States were stretched to the Pacific Ocean.

### Zachary Taylor
### 1849–1850 (16 months)

**VP:** Millard Fillmore
**Party:** Whig
**State:** Louisiana
**Married:** Margaret Smith
**Lived:** 1784–1850

General Zachary Taylor was called "Old Rough and Ready." He never voted—until his own election! His horse, Whitey, grazed on the White House lawn. He died after a Fourth of July celebration.

### Millard Fillmore
### 1850–1853
**VP:** None
**Party:** Whig
**State:** New York
**Married:** Abigail Powers (d. 1853); Caroline McIntosh
**Lived:** 1800 – 1874

Millard Fillmore read the dictionary during breaks as a young mill worker. He was a representative from New York. His wife Abigail started the Presidential Library in the oval room at the White House.

### Franklin Pierce
### 1853–1857
**VP:** William Rufus De Vane King
**Party:** Democratic
**State:** New Hampshire
**Married:** Jane Appleton
**Lived:** 1804 – 1869

General Franklin Pierce was a representative and senator from New Hampshire. When he took office, he was the youngest President up to that time—age 48.

## James Buchanan
## 1857–1861

**VP:** John C. Breckinridge
**Party:** Democratic
**State:** Pennsylvania
**Married:** Never married
**Lived:** 1791 – 1868

James Buchanan was the only President who never married; his niece Harriet Lane served as First Lady. He was a senator from Pennsylvania. His eyes were unusual: one was near-sighted, the other far-sighted.

## Abraham Lincoln
## 1861–1865

**VP:** Hannibal Hamlin;
Andrew Johnson
**Party:** Republican (National Union)
**State:** Illinois
**Married:** Mary Todd
**Lived:** 1809 – 1865

Abraham Lincoln, "Honest Abe," served during the War Between the States (Civil War) and declared that all slaves were to be free. He was the first President to be assassinated. His face is on the penny and the five-dollar bill. At 6 feet 4 inches tall, he was the tallest President.

### Andrew Johnson
### 1865–1869

**VP:** None
**Party:** Democratic (National Union)
**State:** Tennessee
**Married:** Eliza McCardle
**Lived:** 1808–1875

Andrew Johnson was a tailor before he became a senator and governor of Tennessee. While he was President, the United States bought the territory of Alaska from Russia.

### Ulysses S. Grant
### 1869–1877

**VP:** Schuyler Colfax;
Henry Wilson
**Party:** Republican
**State:** Ohio
**Married:** Julia Dent
**Lived:** 1822–1885

General Ulysses S. Grant was the commander of the United States Army. Born Hiram Ulysses Grant, he never liked his H.U.G. initials. At West Point he was incorrectly enrolled as Ulysses S. Grant—and he kept the name!

# Rutherford Birchard Hayes
## 1877–1881

**VP:** William Almon Wheeler
**Party:** Republican
**State:** Ohio
**Married:** Lucy Webb
**Lived:** 1822 – 1893

General Rutherford Hayes was a governor from Ohio. He signed a bill that allowed female lawyers to argue cases before the Supreme Court.

# James Abram Garfield
## 1881 (6½ months)

**VP:** Chester Alan Arthur
**Party:** Republican
**State:** Ohio
**Married:** Lucretia Rudolph
**Lived:** 1831 – 1881

General James Garfield was called "The Preacher President." He was a representative from Ohio. He was the first left-handed President. He was the second President to be assassinated.

## Chester Alan Arthur
## 1881–1885

**VP:** None
**Party:** Republican
**State:** New York
**Married:** Ellen Herndon
**Lived:** 1829 – 1886

Chester Arthur became President upon the death of Garfield. During the last years of his term, he was very sick with a kidney disease—but he kept it a secret.

## Grover Cleveland
## 1885–1889

**VP:** Thomas A. Hendricks
**Party:** Democratic
**State:** New York
**Married:** Frances Folsom
**Lived:** 1837 – 1908

Grover Cleveland was a governor of New York. He was the first President to get married in the White House. He is the only President who served terms that were years apart.

### Benjamin Harrison
### 1889–1893
**VP:** Levi P. Morton
**Party:** Republican
**State:** Indiana
**Married:** Caroline Scott (d. 1892);
Mary Dimmick
**Lived:** 1833–1901

General Benjamin Harrison was the grandson of the 9th President. He was a senator from Indiana. He became President 100 years after the very first President— George Washington.

### Grover Cleveland
### 1893–1897
**VP:** Adlai E. Stevenson
**Party:** Democratic
**State:** New York
**Married:** Frances Folsom
**Lived:** 1837–1908

Grover Cleveland was also the 22nd President. He was the first President to have a child born in the White House. His face is on the $1,000 bill—which is no longer used.

## William McKinley, Jr.
## 1897–1901

**VP:** Garret A. Hobart;
Theodore Roosevelt
**Party:** Republican
**State:** Ohio
**Married:** Ida Saxton
**Lived:** 1843 – 1901

William McKinley was a representative and governor from Ohio. He was assassinated just six months into his second term. His face is on the $500 bill—which is no longer used.

## Theodore Roosevelt
## 1901–1909

**VP:** Charles W. Fairbanks
**Party:** Republican
**State:** New York
**Married:** Alice Lee (d. 1884);
Edith Carow
**Lived:** 1858 – 1919

Theodore "Teddy" Roosevelt was an outdoorsman who established five National Parks. When he took office after McKinley's death, he was the youngest President, at 42 years 10 months. He won the 1906 Nobel Peace Prize.

## William Howard Taft
## 1909–1913

**VP:** James S. Sherman
**Party:** Republican
**State:** Ohio
**Married:** Nellie Herron
**Lived:** 1857 – 1930

William Taft—"Big Bill"—was the largest President: 6 feet tall, 300 pounds. As President, he started the federal income tax. He served as Chief Justice of the U.S. Supreme Court.

## Woodrow Wilson
## 1913–1921

**VP:** Thomas R. Marshall
**Party:** Democratic
**State:** New Jersey
**Married:** Ellen Axson (d. 1914);
Edith Galt
**Lived:** 1856 – 1924

Woodrow Wilson—"The Professor"—was the only President to earn a Ph.D. He served during the Great War (World War I). He signed the 19th Amendment, giving women the right to vote. He won the 1919 Nobel Peace Prize.

### 29 Warren Gamaliel Harding
### 1921–1923

**VP:** Calvin Coolidge
**Party:** Republican
**State:** Ohio
**Married:** Florence Kling
**Lived:** 1865–1923

At age 19, Warren Harding ran a newspaper. He was the first President to receive votes from women. In 1922, he was the first President to speak on the radio. He died in office, while traveling back from Alaska.

### 30 Calvin Coolidge
### 1923–1929

**VP:** Charles G. Dawes
**Party:** Republican
**State:** Massachusetts
**Married:** Grace Goodhue
**Lived:** 1872–1933

Calvin Coolidge was born on July 4th! He was a governor of Massachusetts. He took office upon the death of Harding, and was sworn in by a justice of the peace in Vermont—who happened to be his own father.

## Herbert Clark Hoover
### 1929–1933
**VP:** Charles Curtis
**Party:** Republican
**State:** California
**Married:** Lou Henry
**Lived:** 1874–1964

Herbert Hoover was an adventurer and became a multi-millionaire by age 40. He was President at the start of the Great Depression. After his presidency, he was chairman of the Boys' Clubs of America for eight years.

## Franklin Delano Roosevelt
### 1933–1945
**VP:** John N. Garner; Henry A. Wallace; Harry S. Truman
**Party:** Democratic
**State:** New York
**Married:** Eleanor Roosevelt
**Lived:** 1882–1945

Franklin Roosevelt was a 5th cousin of the 26th President. He suffered from polio at age 39, and never walked unaided again. He was President during World War II. He was elected four times and served longer than any President —12 years 1 month. His face is on the dime.

## Harry S. Truman
## 1945–1953

**VP:** Alben W. Barkley
**Party:** Democratic
**State:** Missouri
**Married:** Bess Wallace
**Lived:** 1884 – 1972

Harry Truman had no middle name—he added the "S." He was a senator from Missouri. A sign on his desk read "The Buck Stops Here." He served during the end of World War II.

## Dwight David Eisenhower
## 1953–1961

**VP:** Richard M. Nixon
**Party:** Republican
**State:** Pennsylvania
**Married:** Mamie Doud
**Lived:** 1890 – 1969

General Dwight Eisenhower, nicknamed "Ike," was Commander of Allied Forces in Europe during World War II. He was the first President to serve after the 50th state was added to the union.

## 35 John Fitzgerald Kennedy
### 1961–1963

**VP:** Lyndon B. Johnson
**Party:** Democratic
**State:** Massachusetts
**Married:** Jacqueline Bouvier
**Lived:** 1917 – 1963

John Kennedy—"J.F.K."—was the first Catholic President, the first to be born after 1900, and the youngest to be **elected**. His book, *Profiles in Courage*, won the Pulitzer Prize. He was assassinated in Dallas. His face is on the 50-cent coin.

## 36 Lyndon Baines Johnson
### 1963–1969

**VP:** None; Hubert H. Humphrey
**Party:** Democratic
**State:** Texas
**Married:** Claudia "Lady Bird" Taylor
**Lived:** 1908 – 1973

Lyndon Johnson—"L.B.J."—was a teacher, a rancher, and a senator from Texas. He took the oath of office while aboard the presidential jet, *Air Force One*, upon the death of Kennedy. In 1964, Johnson signed the Civil Rights Act into law.

## Richard Milhous Nixon
## 1969–1974

**VP:** Spiro T. Agnew;
Gerald R. Ford
**Party:** Republican
**State:** California
**Married:** Thelma "Pat" Ryan
**Lived:** 1913 – 1994

Richard Nixon was a senator from California. He was President when the first man walked on the moon. He was accused of being involved in an illegal cover-up, and was the first President to resign from office.

## Gerald Rudolph Ford, Jr.
## 1974–1977

**VP:** Nelson A. Rockefeller
**Party:** Republican
**State:** Michigan
**Married:** Elizabeth "Betty" Bloomer
**Lived:** 1913 – 2006

Gerald Ford turned down a contract with the National Football League. He was a representative from Michigan for 25 years. He was appointed Vice President, and then became President when Nixon resigned—so he was never actually elected into office.

## James "Jimmy" Earl Carter, Jr.
### 1977–1981

**39**

**VP:** Walter Mondale
**Party:** Democratic
**State:** Georgia
**Married:** Rosalynn Smith
**Lived:** 1924–Present

Jimmy Carter was called "The Peanut President" because his family had run a peanut farm. He was a governor of Georgia. After his term, he won the 2002 Nobel Peace Prize.

## Ronald Wilson Reagan
### 1981–1989

**40**

**VP:** George H.W. Bush
**Party:** Republican
**State:** California
**Married:** Jane Wyman;
Nancy Davis
**Lived:** 1911–2004

Ronald Reagan was an actor, who appeared in 53 films, and a governor of Califonia. He was wounded in an assassination attempt, and joked, "I forgot to duck." He was the oldest President when he left office at 77 years 11 months.

### 41 George Herbert Walker Bush
### 1989–1993

**VP:** Dan Quayle
**Party:** Republican
**State:** Texas
**Married:** Barbara Pierce
**Lived:** 1924–Present

George H.W. Bush was U.S. Ambassador to the United Nations and Director of the CIA. He was President during the Persian Gulf War. He is the father of the 43rd President.

### 42 William Jefferson Clinton
### 1993–2001

**VP:** Albert Gore, Jr.
**Party:** Democratic
**State:** Arkansas
**Married:** Hillary Rodham
**Lived:** 1946–Present

William "Bill" Clinton was a saxophone player and had thought about becoming a professional musician. He was governor of Arkansas at age 32. He was President during the launch of the first White House website.

### George Walker Bush
### 2001–2009
**VP:** Richard Bruce Cheney
**Party:** Republican
**State:** Texas
**Married:** Laura Welch
**Lived:** 1946–Present

George W. Bush is the son of the 41st President. He was a manager of the Texas Rangers baseball team and a governor of Texas. He was President during the terrorist attacks of September 11, 2001, and the war in Iraq.

### Barack Hussein Obama II
### 2009–2017
**VP:** Joseph R. Biden, Jr.
**Party:** Democratic
**State:** Illinois
**Married:** Michelle Robinson
**Lived:** 1961–Present

Barack Obama was the first African-American President. His father was from Kenya, and his mother was from Kansas. He was a senator from Illinois. He won the 2009 Nobel Peace Prize.

## Donald John Trump
## 2017–Present

**VP:** Michael Pence
**Party:** Republican
**State:** New York
**Married:** Ivana Zelníčková;
Marla Maples; Melania Knauss
**Lived:** 1942–Present

Donald Trump was a real estate developer and businessman, hosting and producing the T.V. show *The Apprentice*. He is the wealthiest President, worth more than all the other Presidents combined.

# Prez Quiz!

1) Who was the youngest person to hold the office of President?

2) Who was the youngest person to be *elected* President?

3) Who was the oldest President? The shortest? The tallest? The biggest?

4) Who was the first President to live in the White House?

5) Who was the first President to have a child born in the White House?

6) Which Presidents died on July 4th?

7) Which President was born on July 4th?

8) Which Presidents had sons who became President?

9) Which Presidents won the Nobel Peace Prize?

**ANSWERS:** 1) Theodore Roosevelt; 2) John F. Kennedy; 3) Ronald Reagan, James Madison, Abraham Lincoln, William Taft; 4) John Adams; 5) Grover Cleveland; 6) John Adams, Thomas Jefferson, James Monroe; 7) Calvin Coolidge; 8) John Adams (John Quincy Adams), George H.W. Bush (George W. Bush); 9) Theodore Roosevelt, Woodrow Wilson, Jimmy Carter, Barack Obama